Invocation and Activation of The Seal

With this seal of dissolution, I activate the internal, adversarial power of Satan within my Self. I call upon the power to cause the change that is needed in my life. May this dissolution free me from the things I no longer want or need. And may I invoke the powers of change, wisdom, intuition, and strength to manifest within. All is love and freedom, in Satan's name.

Tasa Reme Laris Satan- Ave Satanas

Divine

Meditations

Ψ

M. King

Divine Meditations

Mastering the Darkness Within

Ψ

M. King

DB PUBLISHING 2016

MMXVI

DB Publishing is an arm of Darkerwood Publishing Group, PO Box 2011, Arvada, CO 80001.

ISBN: 978-1535177283

Book Design by Stephanie Reisner
Editorial: Tenebrae Accedit, T. Jenkins
Cover by Prism

Acknowledgments

To Steph, as always thanks for all the mentorship, support, motivation and inspiration you have given to me. Your words of wisdom have helped me develop magickally and spiritually in a massive way.

I would like to give special thanks to Andy Norman, Lee Priestley, Dan Dean, Janet, Marcellus Maynes, Miguel Branas, Azrow Moore III, and Corrina Hicks. I'm blessed enough to have crossed paths with you all. With that, I would like to thank you for the initiations and lessons. To the members of the Order of the Hidden Rose, Temple of the Ascending Flame, and the Temple of Atem, may our bonds continue to grow strong over time.

To my mother, Annette King, and sister, Shannon Clark; Your moral support and unconditional love have become a foundational part of my life, and for that, I am forever in your debt.

I would like to give special thanks to E.A. Koetting, Edgar Kerval, and Asenath Mason. Your individual works have inspired me greatly to push the boundaries on my personal spirituality. I have been able to test my limits because of your influence.

I would like to give my sincerest thanks to the many gods, goddesses, angels, demons, geniuses and ancestors that have assisted me on my path. I would like to give special attention to Ashtaroth (Ashtoreth), my Matron, and Venus. Because of these two amazing Daemons, I have been able to create the life with the people that I love through their influence and guidance.

To Belphagor, thank you for all the energy, motivation, and guidance you have provided me during this project. Although I stayed up toiling away until the wee hours of the night, I'm sure that I will have great success with it thanks to you.

HO DRAKON HO MEGAS

Introduction

TO DARE

(Ayar Secore On Ca Eurynomous)

"Divine Meditations: Mastering The Darkness Within" is a guide that will explore the aspects of activating the light within the darkness. I plan to walk the practitioner through a Daemonolater's perspective of activating inner gnosis, which can only happen by venturing into the dark and abyssal nature in which we were all created, aligning you with the divine state of GOD.

I encourage each practitioner to submerge themselves completely without giving it a second thought. The information that this book contains is comprised of very personal and intimate meditation techniques revealed to me with the assistance of the Daemonic Divine. Through their guidance, I can deliver to you a few different ways of approaching your ascent, all this achieved without complex methods, utilizing the very natures of inner light and inner darkness. In this aspect, I have been blessed to have had one on one conversations and instruction from the Daemonic, revealing step by step methods of very intense and powerful techniques, all of which I have been privy to learn and share with you, the reader. Although they may come across as very basic methods, they will still prove to aid you on your path none the less.

The techniques within these pages will prove to be an initiation in and of itself. As you progress through each and every step, you will notice a change that begins to take place. At first, this may appear to be just coincidence. But as you travel further along, you will prove to yourself that there is, indeed, something more happening beneath the surface.

The best description I could provide for this entire process is "dissolution,". an alchemical term used to describe the breaking down of one element to change it to the next. A metaphorical death if you will. Letting go of the old to welcome the new. These descriptions I think fits perfectly with the work involved. Because death is what you will be experiencing, breaking down what or who you thought you were, to become something more.

Provided, will be a few meditation techniques to practice. Feel free to choose one that works for you. I do, however, suggest that each meditation be performed over a period of seven to nine days. This ensures that the practitioner unlocks whatever hidden knowledge that may need to surface. This process also guarantees that you will come to an understanding of how and why the technique works for you. Seven to nine days is a good amount of time to create a snowball effect of changes in the energies invoked. Giving them a chance to work for and with you.

I will say, dear reader, to make sure that you approach this work with intent to give your all. Doing so will increase your chances of enjoying the benefits in the end.

I would like to highlight that this is a book of practicality, meaning that it was written with the intent to be used. Not to be placed on the bookshelf, collecting dust and soon forgotten. I've chosen to stay away from long-winded historical facts and theory. Not that I have anything against history or theory at all. I think that sometimes it creates a distraction from the actual work. Skipping the wordiness also prevents me from wasting your time and energy.

However, feel free to do any additional research on Daemonolatry on your own. There will be a list of books included in the bibliography. You will also notice that at the beginning of each section, I've placed certain Daemonic enns along with the titles. I've done this on purpose, mainly to help prepare you, the reader, with the changes that are about to take place. This change will occur through the Daemon heading each section.

These Daemonic forces will start to open you up to experience your personal gnosis. But outside of the obvious enns, I have withheld from placing blinds or encrypted messages inside the material. I feel that if you are willing to do this type of work, then it is because it's something that you may need in your life at this time. And mostly, because you are advanced enough to handle any hiccups that may occur.

Finally, the main intent of this guide is to assist you, (the practitioner), with methods of creating and causing a real change in your life. I will suggest not using this manual lightly. These methods do have the potential to be incredibly intense and powerful so do take care when working with them.

What to Expect

I can confidently say, that while performing the work within this guide, you are bound to unlock the hidden gnosis within yourself. Whether voluntarily or involuntarily, change will happen. This change is only natural when working with the Daemonic. Once the change does start to take place, it's hard to hold onto those things you no longer need in your life. That is the main focus of these techniques. These methods were gathered through various means of ascension work, breathing, visualization, chanting, etc. It will involve all of the human faculty's necessary to make the techniques work for you as an individual.

I, with a few other individuals, have taken the time out to work with these methods to assure their effectiveness. I can happily admit that the results were indeed very potent. Although some of the results were a pain for me to experience, they were totally worth it. You will find an eclectic mix of techniques here, from chakra work, to enns that summon the Old Gods, to powerful visualizations that will instantaneously affect you, on many levels.

This chapbook will deliver to you a variety of tools needed to become a more balanced, self-realized, conscious God/Goddess that exists in the here and now, all while dissolving and destroying the old you in the process.

I do understand that there is a multitude of grimoires, meditation guides, and spiritual manuals that promise the practitioner change and conscious awakening only to disappoint. I have made sure to put forth the maximum amount of effort to fulfill the expectations presented in this work. However, do keep in mind that in order to create desired changes, work will need to be done. Never overlook time and effort that is needed to create the results that you're intending.

Safety Precautions

As with any intensive Daemonic work, a few words of caution are necessary for the unsuspecting practitioner. Where I wish nothing more than for the reader to experience all that this grimoire has to offer, I do feel that it is somewhat of my responsibility, to prepare you for working with the energies this intensively. As most may know, doing any inner alchemical work is never really something that takes place overnight, it takes time. This is why patience is key throughout your practice. It's usually not until you look back and notice what has taken place that you realize that hindsight is key.

The techniques included here aim at unlocking and mastering those hidden energies that have been lying dormant within you all this time. I have aimed my focus mainly on bringing those energies to the surface so that you may come to balance them within your life. I have noticed that our society is set on moving in a direction that separates our lunar and solar natures, making it a challenge to create some balance between them.

My ultimate intent is to focus on bringing those energies back into a state of balance and harmony. Ultimately, bringing you into a state of awareness. However, this can only be done by awakening and releasing these hidden energies deep inside.

As mentioned before, patience is key. I do want you to make the progress needed for your spiritual growth, but I also want to express how important it is to take your time in doing so. I mention this because I have experienced firsthand what happens when you overdo things due to impatience and anxiousness. Things become very chaotic, causing an overload of changes that you may not be ready to deal with. I know this well from taking on tons of Daemonic work at the same time. Thinking I was totally prepared, some of the experiences proved otherwise.

Granted, the work I performed did bring about great success in my life, but it did test my limits, often making me feel overwhelmed. So take my advice and be patient my friends. Added to this, you also want to make sure that you are getting plenty of rest and drinking plenty of fluids, at least while doing this work. As many of you know with extended spiritual or magickal work, physical, mental, and spiritual exhaustion sometimes occurs. By making sure that you are well rested and hydrated, you are increasing your chances of having a more successful, balanced session. I will go into this in more detail as you read further along.

The bottom line is that it's important for you to know your limits. It's natural to want to push yourself to the end and not think twice about it. However, with this type of work, it is very important to know when you have reached those limits. Hopefully, you are sensitive or aware enough to know when you should take a rest or stop. If, while doing this work, you feel you have reached a point that you can't handle what is transpiring, stop. Take a rest and pick up where you left off last. There will always be another day to come back to it.

Keep in mind, that above all your health is the most important thing here. This is not a race, and no one is judging you on how far or how fast you can progress through these pages. So if you have to put the book down and come back to it days, weeks, months, or even years later then that's all right. You and I both know that you would rather be safe than sorry. And with that, I welcome you to Divine Meditations: Mastering the Darkness within.

~M. King

Part1: Preparation

Ascending Darkness

TO KNOW

(Renich tasa uberaca biasa icar Lucifer)

As I stated above, the methods in this book will plunge you into a sea of darkness, pushing you towards spiritual evolution. A few of these methods focus on taking you directly to the heart of internal darkness. Here, you will come face to face with forces and energies that have been buried deep within you since the beginning of time.

As you come into contact with this current, you will learn to let go and let it devour you, rebirthing you into true light. Now my intent is by no means to make this grimoire sound all "scary and spooky." I am just revealing to you what has worked for me on my personal path while working with these energies.

As many of you know, there is a variety of ways one can ascend to God/Goddesshood. I think that working with the

Daemonic divine is by far one of the best ways to achieve this. Through experience, I have been taught very valuable lessons, all the while testing my personal limits each time. Each time, coming out stronger and wiser.

I will admit, one of the best attributes of the Daemonic is that they amplify the emotions, energies and thoughts that you carry, intensifying each ritual working that much more. After a while, you learn to embrace this and allow it to help you break through obstacles that stand in your way, including fear.

Embracing Darkness

I used to find the thought of being in complete darkness terrifying, especially after having to experience being locked away in total darkness for an extended period of time. One day, at the age of 10, my cousins thought that it would be funny to lock me in their basement as a practical joke. This terrified me on many levels throughout my childhood. This experience became very traumatizing and dramatic.

From that point, it took me years to build up enough courage to step into a dark room. Eventually, I managed to get over this challenge through personal courage and internal strength. When I first started out on the path of magick, it was much like being stuck in my cousin's basement; Being forced to come face to face with what seemed to be an impending darkness with an initial feeling of fear and often leaving me feeling lost and confused.

The real remedy didn't come until I came across various magicians, such as S. Connolly, E.A. Koetting, Edgar Kerval, Asenath Mason, and my very close friend Marcellus. Through their works, words, and examples, I was able to gain some understanding of how to steer safely and carefully through the seas of chaos. All the while, helping me to push past obstacles that prevented me from progressing forward in life, and empowering me on so many levels.

When I had chosen to embrace this particular path in life, I felt it was important enough to tell my friends and family. Although feeling very reluctant to do so, I did it anyway. It often followed with silence, looks of confusion, or fear. The advice I received the most was to "Stay away from the dark path and only to stick with the light" and "If you follow the dark path you will eventually go mad." This was often confusing to me, because to my understanding, the true path of the occultist and magus has always been about bringing balance into one's life.

A balance that is brought about through a dark gnosis transformed into light enabling the practitioner to harmonize the "light" and "dark" energies within oneself. But, to my surprise, that's not how it is. To many, the path of light is to be embraced fully, and the path of darkness is to be avoided, at all costs.

I have practiced Tai Chi for many years. One of the core philosophies that stands out above all others is that one cannot know one's self until they learn to harmonize their inner yin and yang. You learn from day one that there can truly be no light without darkness and vice versa. This concept of polarity is so important that it seeps into our daily lives in many ways, except it's subtle. At the very moment when I was warned to avoid this path of darkness, no matter what, it became my apple, much like the fruit that tempted Eve in Eden.

Ultimately, this motivated me to find out why this path seemed to be so dangerous. It wasn't until I took the plunge into the oceans of darkness and chaos that I finally figured out why so many fear this path. I've learned that many practitioners are afraid of facing themselves. They resist letting the ego-self die, even if only for a moment. I eventually came to the realization that, the keys to survival on this path are to 1) never resist or run from the energies, and 2) explore things on your own before you take anyone's advice. This led me to some of my greatest lessons.

Many people are afraid of coming face to face with themselves. Most prevent the dissolution of the ego to take place, instead of accepting and living in balance with their dark nature. Many have avoided it as if it's something that is evil and horrid, when it should be the exact opposite, it should be embraced. This is why within this grimoire I throw you head first into the seas of darkness and chaos so that you eventually come to an understanding that you must embrace all aspects of yourself to be complete.

It's like what I have been told so many times before in my past "if you swim against the current you will surely be pulled under and devoured by it." My suggestion to the reader is to step outside of your comfort zone, give into this current and allow it to transform you. You will be better off for it in the long run.

Steadying of the Mind

While involved in this type of work it is very easy to get lost in the ecstasy of change, forgetting why you have started the work in the first place. It's very important to have a few preliminary goals set aside before performing your first ritual or meditation. Doing this will help aim and push the energies towards what changes are needed in your life.

Now, more often than not, the spirits will most likely tweak your goals and intention in a way that will manifest what you need, and if this happens go with it. The key is to stay focused no matter what, and the fact that you have to increase your focus is growth in and of itself.

Shattering of the Spirit

When starting this type of work, you will notice that you may not feel like yourself, or that something is out of sync. This is nothing more than the decomposition and transmutation of the spirit, the very core of who you are is beginning to change. Because you may not be used to doing work of this intensity, it may take you some time to reach a level of balance, but that's ok because it will happen eventually.

I have always found that the more challenging the work, the more likely you will gain some benefit from it. I've also noticed that the more you try to hang onto poisonous or hindering habits the more painful the transition would be. It's at these most vital points of temporary pain and suffering that you come to a conclusion. The conclusion is that for you to step forward in your life, these feelings, sensations, emotions, habits and thoughts must die. They must become nothing more than a faded memory.

However, be warned that once you have opened Pandora's Box, there is no closing it, the energies that have been activated must run their course until completion. The best thing to do at this point would be to go along with the flow with little to no resistance as possible.

This process can be very challenging and also very beautiful all at the same time. Just know that you are putting effort into something that you will reap amazing benefits from. With that being said, while the spirits and abyssal energies are deconstructing and reconstructing you, know that you are becoming a better magician, spiritualist and human for it.

Awakening the Inner-Deity

TO WILL

(Tasa reme laris Satan- ave Satanis)

Once the work is complete, and all things are said and done, you will experience a new sense of freedom. The inner deity will awaken, and you will be born anew facing this reality with a new found sense of power, giving you all that you need to take control of your life and do with it as you will. Others will notice the inner fires of life and gnosis burning brightly inside of you.

You will see things in a new light, no longer feeling a sense of aversion for what is dark and hidden, but embracing it as a part of all existence. The God-forms that I have chosen to include here are ones that will assist you in making sure that you take the necessary steps to create the change in your life that you desire. They will lend you their strength, wisdom, courage and abilities.

But with that being said make sure that you give these forces the respect that they deserve. Nothing's worse than trying to give someone assistance to only have them treat you like crap. Treat the spirits as you would like to be treated. Now I'm not saying that you have to grovel before the spirits or even beg. All I'm saying is to do your best to keep that ego in check. If you keep your ego in check and come from an angle of respect, I guarantee that you will be successful in your workings.

Besides, one thing that I've learned from working with the spirits, Daemons, in particular, is that they reflect the energy and intention of the practitioner right back at them. So if you humble yourself you will get very far with amazing results, but if you come across as arrogant and bossy then be prepared to fall on your face, hard.

Once you have gone through the techniques and have completed the work (at your pace), you will come to a realization that, the inner God/Goddess has always been active in your life all this time. You will realize that it only took for you to move out of your way to see it. Once you reconnect to the inner light, be prepared to tap into the direct current that flows through all things making manifesting things in your life that much easier. Because of this understanding, things will have no choice but to fall into place for you.

These methods have the ability to empower you, revealing a life that reaches a peak of joy, understanding, and balance instead of despair, pain, and suffering. With all things said, keep in mind that you will have to travel through the darkness to reach the light on the other side.

The Light of GOD

This is a topic that I read or hear about quite often. Usually, it's within the realm of what the light (or essence) of God truly is. What I will usually say in response to this subject is, no man can judge another man's experience, meaning that what you may experience throughout your life as God will be completely different to what I or anyone else may have personally experienced. We can only share stories of what it felt like, what effects may have taken place, and what we have been lucky to have revealed to us.

Although this is easier said than done, it's up to you as an individual to let go of comparisons and to use your intuition to discover what God's light is to you. Overall, what we can all agree upon is that the light of God is, in a sense, complete freedom within. It is some divine activation that gives us the ability to move beyond what we consider to be "normal". We can also say that the light of God releases the tethers in your life that may have hindered your growth in becoming a realized God Being.

The thing about the light of God, the source, the ALL, the Creator is that it is found in both pure, benevolent light and also within abyssal darkness. Since God itself is the ALL, there is no separation on how one can achieve spiritual awakening. I would like you to keep these things in mind as you perform these meditations, remembering that divine realization could be activated at any point in time as you work through the steps presented here.

Methods of Ascension

I have taken the liberty of providing several different techniques in which you will be using to incorporate all the senses. The techniques involve all of the possible modalities and sub-modalities within the human system. As I have stated before, there are no set or particular ways to ascend on your personal path, and these methods will make sure that you ascend in the best way possible.

I have known people to reach these high levels of understanding and ascension through reading, breathing, chanting, singing, contacting spirits, etc. you name it, and it has been done to reach the next level of one's personal spiritual growth. These methods will also prevent any pigeonholing of fellow magicians, occultists or spiritualists in any way. I know that I, personally, work best through visualization, visualization of my deities, and visualization of the effects, and so on. But this doesn't mean that the same rules apply to you.

I do suggest that if you can't find a particular modality that suits you try working with them all. Unleash your inner creativity towards your ascension it will add an element of fun to your workings. This also prevents you from taking your path too serious. Below I have included just some of the methods that will aid you while you perform each working.

Invocations:

Just know that in Daemonolatry, we always invoke the Daemonic forces to join us and aid in ritual. Invocation has proven for many years to be the most respectful way of working with the Daemonic. By invoking, you are requesting the presence of the Daemonic divine. It's common to invoke the four Daemonic kings along with Satan or the head of your pantheon within the ritual space.

With invocation, the practitioner will use an incantation, enn or a simple request to welcome the Daemonic into the ritual space. By no means do we ever force spirits to appear through invocation. To be honest, that's just not how Daemonolaters work.

Evocation:

In Daemonolatry, we don't by any means evoke spirits to appear before us, because it usually means to force the presence of the Daemonic against its will to appear in the space and since we approach them from an angle of respect, it would go against everything that we teach.

Sigils:

Calling cards of the spirits, sigils have been used for a very long time whether in Ceremonial Magick, Satanism, Daemonolatry or traditional Voodoo (veves). You will be hard pressed not to find the use of sigils to get into contact with the spirits on the other side in any magickal, religious or spiritual system. With that being said, I have included several sigils that connect to the Daemonic directly.

These sigils have been added here either by courtesy of S. Connolly or as I have received them through personal communication. This also means that some sigils may have a very raw appearance without being cleaned up or edited. I do believe that there is power in sigils that have very archaic looking shapes and appearances. To me, they hold a direct link to the subconscious and trigger the hidden energies inside of us all.

Incantations and Enns:

These are verbal invocations that will draw forth the essence of spirits and even draw forth sacred energies that drive your body. There is a great power in the spoken word, and here you will be harnessing that power to help you ascend.

The enns and incantations should be vibrated to have the best effect, meaning you should let the energies of each word radiate from your entire body as you speak them. This is because you are putting life into the words, as you do so you are activating the power within.

Breathing:

The cornerstone of our techniques will be based on driving the energy throughout the body with the breath. It is strongly believed that the breath connects the spirit to the physical, and I agree with this wholeheartedly. The breath will act as a vehicle to drive the intent and focus of what you are trying to achieve. You will be putting a lot of focus on breathing correctly throughout the various techniques here.

Seating Positions:

Even though it is usually suggested that you sit in the most comfortable position you can manage, the most important thing is always to make sure that your back and spine are as straight as possible and that you don't bend the neck forward. I suggest that you tuck the chin in without craning the neck. This can be done while sitting in a chair or sitting on the floor. There will be no need to sit in a full lotus or half-lotus position unless you desire to do so.

Skrying:

Through reflective sources, we can see into the subconscious mind, and push ourselves into an ascended state to converse with the Daemonic, although, it does help if you have a knack for using this form of clairvoyant skill, one could still try this method to see if it could be developed at all.

Ritual Setup

Setting up your ritual space can be as simple or as intricate as you prefer it to be. However, there are a few tools that I suggest having to aid you in your workings. They are as follows:

Ritual Blade - Being the staple of any Magicians repertoire, the ritual blade has several purposes from invocation, drawing blood, protecting one's self against wily or harmful spirits. If you don't have one already, I would suggest buying an inexpensive one at your local sporting goods store. Or, if you just can't afford to purchase a blade at the time, a kitchen knife would work just as well. Even your pointer and middle finger could suffice if need be.

Diabetic Lancets - If you have read any of S. Connolly's material you will always come across her suggesting the purchase of a diabetic lancet with disposable needles. This is great for drawing blood in the least harmful or destructive way possible.

Just remember to grab a sharps container to dispose of your used needles. Diabetic lancets are one of the most sanitary ways to go about gathering blood that's needed.

Parchment Paper - Used for painting, burning sigils, making a request and all sorts. You will most likely work your way through quite a few sheets in no time; I suggest buying, at least, a pack of 100 Sheets to keep at the ready.

An assortment of colored candles - I suggest having a collection of candles of several different colors, especially black candles. Tapered candles are an excellent choice and will be great during your meditation sessions, they will help to focus your attention. You could even try your hand at using unmarked glass seven-day candles that they sell mostly at any local botanica.

These type of candles are great if you are tight on money and can't afford to buy candles in bulk. If you do choose to use tapered candles, make sure that you have candle holders as well.

Scrying Device - Now whether this is a black bowl filled with water, a scrying mirror or even a crystal orb, you want to have at least one device around. The scrying device is for communing with the Daemonic Divine or tapping into the deeper recesses of the subconscious mind.

Incense - A great tool to have when you are inducing an environment that will invite the spirits or invoke a specific energy within yourself. There is a lot of power in scent that's often overlooked nowadays. They are also great to have around during any ritual work that you're doing. And who am I kidding they can smell pretty awesome too.

Oils/Oleums - Oleums and Oils are great for anointing yourself to inducing altered states of ascension especially when the mixtures prepared correctly. They can also be used to anoint various objects such as candles, talismans, seals, etc.

Clay - For molding and sculpting items such as talismans, vessels, artifacts, etc.

Circle Constructs

Circle constructs are important as they aid in creating a potent and conducive environment that is inviting to the Daemonic. They can be created and performed in several different ways, but for now, we will just stick with a traditional elemental construct. I've decided to add the Daemonolatry based elemental circle to this grimoire to help you amplify the energy of the space.

This type of circle also enhances the communication between the practitioner and the Daemonic, while also creating a comfortable space in which the practitioner feels balanced and the daemonic are welcomed respectfully.

Key points to remember when invoking the Daemonic:

1. Don't demand, be aggressive or arrogant with the Daemonic

2. Do not by any means stab your blade or fingers in the air.

These types of methods may work with other forms of magical or spiritual paths but is not conducive to working any Daemonolatry based ritual.

The ZD/DZ sigil that's drawn in the air while stating each Daemonic enn

Invoking Lucifer

Start by facing the eastern portion of the temple, take your blade or fingers and draw the ZD sigil in the air in front of you. As you do so vibrate the enn: (*Renich tasa uberaca biasa icar Lucifer*).

Invoking Flareous

Move to the south portion of the temple and draw the ZD sigil and vibrate (*Ganic tasa fubin Flareous*).

Invoking Leviathan

Move to the western portion of the temple, draw the ZD sigil and vibrate (*Jedan tasa hoet naca Leviathan*).

Invoking Belial

Move to the north portion of the temple and vibrate (*Lirach tasa vefa welhc Belial*).

Invoking Satan

Finally, step to the center of the temple and invoke Satan by vibrating (*Tasa reme laris Satan*). Satan, in a classical Daemonolatry sense, represents the All.

To close the circle, you would give a license to depart by moving counter-clockwise, give thanks to the Daemonic Divine and return to normal consciousness.

(Do keep in mind that if you have other elementals that you have chosen to work with, by all means feel free to invoke them instead. This includes the head of your pantheon or All.)

Preparation of the Practitioner

Preparation is important in mostly anything that you do, especially in the areas of magic and spirituality. You don't want to jump into this haphazardly especially if you are new to this type of stuff. I'm sure you have heard the saying that proper preparation prevents piss-poor results. This applies here. You want to take all the necessary steps to aid in your success with little to no hiccups. Even though I believe that a good portion of our failures are in the mentality we have, it doesn't mean that things outside of ourselves can't have an equally powerful effect on us just as well.

However, we can't ignore the fact that in all actuality, preparation begins in the mind and it then leads to physical action. Here are a few things that you can do to help set the mood, so to speak, to work with the Daemonic.

Baths or Showers - This is a good way to remove any gunk (physical, spiritual or astral) that you may have picked up throughout your day. There's a lot of power in the element of water. A good visualization to include would be as you wash, to visualize, feel, hear, or sense that as the water is washing over you, it is removing any traces of negative energy attached to you.

The mucky water is then washed away exiting via the water drain. This technique can be performed in whatever method or fashion you choose. I found this to be a very powerful technique to use after a long, complex day at work. It's just something about washing away all the crap that has accumulated in your life that's very soothing.

Kabbalistic, Qlippothic or Daemonic Cross - I have modified this technique a bit. You will find the original method in *"The Kasdeya Rite of Ba'al."* This is a great method for balancing the energy levels within the body, not to mention providing protection as well. This technique is better performed after you have performed the shower technique I have given previously. You would perform this by standing, feet together and arms spread out to the sides. The left palm should be facing downwards while the right palm is facing upwards.

You will then envision the black pillar of severity on the left and the white pillar of mercy on the right. You will then invoke the names and enns of whatever deities that are within your respective pantheon. Begin to visualize them within each and every corresponding sphere that's associated in accordance with the body. So for example, I would personally invoke Ashtaroth at my crown in the sphere of Kether all the way down to Malkuth. And since I am very familiar with Ashtaroth's energies it would be more beneficial just to invoke her energies to balance me. You would do the same thing to invoke the essence of your personal Daemonic forces through each sphere within your middle pillar.

Feel free to replace any Daemonic forces that you are most comfortable with, within your middle path spheres. Once you have vibrated the incantations of the Daemonic energy throughout each sphere, you would then visualize pure white balancing, cleansing energies that are pulsating and flowing up and down the body and across the arms.

You would then envision a sphere of light that forms around the entirety of the body. This technique will bring harmony and balance to the energies in your body. I even recommend using this method daily whether you decide to go into a meditation session or not.

Hydration - As mentioned previously it is important to stay hydrated as it can help prevent you from blacking out and it also acts as an internal purifier flushing out any toxins that may be trapped in your body.

Rest - Also vital to any spiritual and magickal workings, the practitioner must be well rested and have as much energy as possible. If you lack the energy to perform a meditation session, do not proceed, pick back up when you are well rested. You will not gain any real benefit from being tired and attempting to meditate.

Part 2: Divine Meditations

TO EXPERIENCE

(*Aum Kring Kalikaye Namaha*)

Here is where we will get into performing the work. The flavor of the following techniques is both unique and eclectic. I believe in keeping things fresh and different. Hopefully, you will benefit from the methods that I have included here. As with any of my works, nothing I ever provide is set in stone, so feel free to change any method or technique in a way that best suits and benefits you.

What I will say is that I recommend at least keeping the overall arching concept of the methods and using them as a template. To get the best benefits from the meditation consider invoking an elemental circle before doing the meditation. I suggest practicing each technique for over a period of seven days. This will attune your energies to the methods given.

NOTE: All sigils have been included towards the back of the book

; Darkness

o me during ascension; this technique will help
to the inner darkness that resides within. I suggest
technique as a primer before you go into the chakra
uissci. n meditation that you will find further along.

In a completely dark room, sit within the space of darkness. Feel this darkness all around you, notice how within the darkness is the loudest silence you've ever heard. While sitting in the darkness, begin visualizing a black sun made of pure dark energy, starting at the very top of your head. Feel the sun's energy radiating and pulsating as it starts to wash over you melting away any stress or tension, relaxing each and every muscle, tendon, and organ. Allow the dark sun's energy to flow over and through every part of your body, from the top of your head to the tips of your toes.

You will then begin to start breathing deeply through the nose, pulling the air down all the way to the very bottom of the lungs, expanding the belly as you do so. As you inhale, visualize the surrounding darkness melting away layers of your body, starting with the flesh. As you exhale through the mouth, deflating the stomach, the flesh fully dissolves away completely. Do this with the flesh, the muscles, the tendons, the bones and the organs until you have finally dissolved away into pure darkness. Once you've achieved this level of awareness, begin breathing in the surrounding dark energy into the space that is now you.

As you breathe in and breathe out, feel the darkness expanding and contracting within and around you, become one with the sensation as it happens. As you breathe in this pattern, you may start to feel a connection linking you to all things in and around you. Embrace this connection, enjoy it, and fall completely into the sensation of oneness with the supreme universal darkness.

After you have reached a point to where you feel satisfied absorbing the darkness around you, began bringing yourself into normal awareness and consciousness. You will start by reversing the process by breathing in and re-absorbing light throughout your entire being. Start by going through the same process of bringing light into yourself as you have done with the darkness around you. Once you feel that you have completely balanced yourself out, complete your meditation and proceed to return to normal consciousness.

-END

Inverse Breathing

This technique is very similar to the becoming darkness method mentioned previously. I have, however, included a difference in the breathing patterns.

Start by sitting in darkness, began relaxing the body through the technique of the dark sun as you've done with the previous meditation. Once the body is relaxed and all tension has melted away, begin breathing in the darkness. Let the darkness fill every part of you, and as this happens, take a few stabilizing, cleansing breaths, allowing the darkness to balance you completely.

Once you feel harmonized within the darkness, start taking deep breaths of the darkness and pull it within you. Inhale for a count of 8 and hold the darkness within for a count of 8. When you exhale, don't exhale the darkness. Instead, you will exhale pure light. See all the light within you expelling from your very core, leaving nothing but infinite abyssal darkness. As the light leaves the space of your body, it is soon devoured by the darkness and dissipates into the space around you. Do this for as long as you can handle it.

After you have done as many breaths as you can manage, began reversing the breathing pattern and start breathing in light and exhaling darkness, all for a count of 8. This will balance the energies within your body.

Once you feel that you are balanced and harmonized, return to normal consciousness. This technique will tire you out or make you extremely light headed, especially if you have never absorbed darkness on this scale before, only to switch the polarity shortly afterward. Once completed with the meditation, take a few moments to ground yourself before moving. Take your time working on this particular technique. *Slow* is the key word here my friends.

*NOTE: You can increase or decrease the breath count if you need to. No need to make yourself uncomfortable to the point of where you lose the focus of the meditation.

-END

Saturnian Sun Meditation

This meditation technique was revealed to me with the assistance of Lucifer. He walked me through each step of transmuting my very essence to become more divine in the process. This technique is one of my favorites because it helps you rediscover your true nature. It also serves as a balancing, purification and protective method in the process. And although this particular method is focused on invoking the inner light instead of darkness, it still proves to be a powerful technique to unlock your inner gnosis.

For this meditation you will need:

- Four yellow candles
- Sigil of Lucifer
- Saturnian Sun Sigil
- Air element based incense

Start by lighting the four yellow candles which are placed at each quarter of the circle. Once done, begin opening the temple with a four quarter ritual construct dedicated to Lucifer. Using an "as above so below" type gesture for all four corners. As you invoke Lucifer, envision that there is a gust of strong wind brushing past your face every time he's invoked.

Feel free to light any incense that has an airy scent to it once you've returned to the original starting point. Anoint the Saturnian Sun sigil, and any sigil related to Lucifer with blood. As you anoint the sigils, visualize them glowing yellow and bright, so bright that the light fills the temple.

Next, sit in the center of the temple facing east. Take a few cleansing deep breaths, aligning yourself to the energy of the temple. Once you feel ready to move forward, close your eyes and visualize that just in front of you, a triangle shaped doorway has formed. This doorway begins to grow bigger and bigger with each breath. It gets big enough to touch the ceiling and floor of the temple simultaneously.

Now see the darkness within the doorway flow into the temple. Let this darkness flow as it will. Now, visualize that in the center of the doorway, the sigil of the Saturnian Sun forms.

The sigil begins to glow brighter and brighter, calling you into the abyss. Let yourself follow this attraction, and flow with it. Let the sigil pull you to the other side. As you are pulled through the abyss, notice the sensations that you have as you travel through. The sensations may be intense; they may be light. Only you will be able to experience what you experience. Either way, just let the sensations happen as they will.

Once you make it to the other side, take a look around, notice the scenery. You may notice that you have entered a space that looks very similar to our very own universe. Take note of the worlds, planets, environments, etc. that surround you, take a moment to drink it all in.

Now take a look in front of you and you will notice that the sigil begins to pull you towards a beam of light that becomes brighter and brighter with each passing second. Soon you will notice that this is a gigantic sun, not like any sun that you've ever seen. This sun appears to be brighter than 10,000 suns and gravity that's heavier than anything you've felt. It has several rings that rotate around it as if it is a lighter version of Saturn. Take your time to soak in this immense power and radiance. Take note of what you're experiencing during this time.

When you're ready, fly/float directly towards the sun and head for the very core. You may notice that you, the temple, or both (you and the temple) begin to heat up. As you travel to the center of the sun, realize that your divine form will prevent you from burning or scorching. Once you make it to the core, sit and absorb the environment and take in the essence, the light, the warmth and support of the sun.

Take it into the very center of you and let this energy flow directly into every strand of DNA, every cell, every pore of your body. After a while you will notice that you began to feel, see, or hear Lucifer. Talk to him and ask him what wisdom he would like to impart to you. Take heed to whatever he reveals to you.

After the communion, spend some time basking in the essence of the Saturnian sun. When you feel you are ready to return to normal consciousness, leave the sun and re-enter through the abyssal doorway. See all the light recede through the door and visualize the door getting smaller and smaller until it's no more. Once you've done this, bring yourself back to consciousness slowly. Give thanks to Lucifer for joining you and close your circle.

-END

Hekate's Poison

Revealed to me during my interactions with Hekate. This meditation is great for invoking a type of spiritual death. I also found this to be a great fear facing exercise.

Ritual Items

- One violet or black candle

- Sigil of Hekate (drawn in purple or black on a white background)

- Offering of red wine for Hekate

Begin by mixing a few drops of blood with the wine, as you do so say Hekate's enn: (*Alora Tasa Hekate Borage et Anana Hekate Ayer At*) over it. Next, invoke the 4 Daemonic kings around the circle and into the space using the ZD sigil. Once you feel that they have arrived, proceed to invoke Hekate, start by facing west and moving clockwise around the circle.

Repeat the incantations in each quadrant of the circle. Once you can feel her presence within the room, return to the center of the circle and vibrate her enn once more. After stating the invocations face northwest, light the single violet candle and begin focusing on her sigil. Place a few drops of blood onto the sigil and begin rhythmically whispering her enn until you feel yourself fall into a trance-like state. After a while you may also notice that her sigil will begin to flash, this is a sure sign that the sigil is activated and that Hekate is present.

Once the sigil is activated, close your eyes and allow yourself to visualize that the entire room is fading away into darkness. The image of the temple is now replaced with the image of a cave entrance. Enter the cave and make your way through to the other side. Take note of what sounds, scents, sights or feelings that occur around you as you journey to the end of the cave.

When you reach the edge of the cave, you may notice that before you a moonlit forest stands. Start making your way through the forest. Within the darkness, you will eventually meet a gnome-like creature who greets you and hands you a vial of liquid to drink. Drink it and take note on how it makes you feel. He will then offer to take you to meet "the lady" deep inside the forest.

Let him lead you through the scenery. Take note of what's around you and what you are experiencing, allowing your consciousness to expand into the environment. You will eventually come to a house within the very heart of the forest. Leave your host and prepare to enter the house. The door has the sigil of Hekate engraved on it. Touch it while saying her enn. The door will open, and you are now allowed to step over the threshold continue to take note of what is transpiring on around you.

Wander around the house to see what things catch your attention. Eventually, Hekate will appear before you and hand you another vial of liquid to drink. This vial contains the poison of Hekate. Make sure to drink it all, leaving nothing behind. Allow the poison to take its effect on you, allow your consciousness to take you further into the meditation. From this point let Hekate guide you.

Take note of any sensations that you experience. Once you have reached a point to where you cannot go any further in your meditation, give thanks to Hekate for joining you, end your meditation, give a license to depart to the Daemonic and return to normal consciousness. -END

Gates of Naamah

This particular meditation was given to me by Naamah, the mother of all succubi. Like the meditation with Hekate, you will experience a spiritual death, which will only last as long as you are willing to fight against the currents of Naamah. I will say that I have grown to fall in love with Naamah and her many dark methods of spiritual transformation. The pain of her initiations is well worth it in the end. This meditation will be broken up into several parts.

For this meditation you will need:

Ritual Items

- Three red candles

- Three black candles

- Two chalices filled with red wine (grape juice will work as well)

- Sigil of Naamah (painted in red on a black background)

- Bloodletting device (or ritual knife)

- Dragons Blood or Sandalwood incense

- Flying Oil or Tiger Balm

- Scrying Device

Pre-invocation

Before Invoking Naamah, anoint your candles with an aphrodisiac oil. While anointing the candles state the enn/invocation of Naamah and envision a fiery red energy flowing into the candles. You will then carve her name into each candle still stating her enn/invocation the entire time. I personally placed one candle South, one Northwest, and one Northeast. Feel free to change this construct in a way that feels right to you.

Make sure there is room enough for you to move around the ritual space as needed. You will then perform the same anointing actions for the three black candles. I decided to place them in a similar triangle fashion facing a south direction. I placed one candle Southeast, one Southwest and one candle facing North. I placed the scrying device in the center of the black candles, the sigil of Naamah was laid in front of the scrying device. Skrying is optional and not necessary to make this ritual work.

First Invocation

Begin by lighting your incense and walking around the circle nine times counter-clockwise, do this while saying the enn/invocation of Naamah: *ic zszszs lia ziatu naamah naamah ziatu*. Envision that waves of red and black energies are starting to fill the space; this energy should flow from the very pit of your belly throughout the rest of your body and enter into the temple. Once you complete the 9th circuit make your way back to the center of the circle.

While sitting within the circle, anoint your 3rd eye and temples with the flying oil or Tiger Balm. Hold your gaze upon Naamah's sigil until it opens up and activates. Once the sigil starts flashing, place a few drops of blood onto it and then begin the first invocation.

- *Oh, Queen of the night, mistress of blood I call you forth.*

- *Temptress of the damned, she who causes carnal pleasures to arise, I invoke thee.*

- Consort of the beast, you who drains forth the life of all caught in your web, enter this temple.

- Naamah the seductress, the one who pleases the nature of the GODS. ARISE!!!

- Oh, sacred queen, come into this temple and fill it with your presence.

- IC ZSZSZS LIA ZIATU NAAMAH NAAMAH ZIATU!!!

When you have completed the first invocation, place a few drops of blood into the chalice of wine that you have set aside for her. Now begin the second invocation.

Second Invocation

- Mother of lust, pleasure, and carnal desire, take up this house.

- She who gives us vision, take up this house.

- Oh grand succubus, partake of my blood that I give of myself to you. Take up this house.

- Consort to Samael, sister to Lilith, take up this house.

- Naamah, enrage my desires, my passions, and my lusts. Let your flames devour me so that I may know you, take up this house.

- Teach and guide me in your ways so that I may become wise to all that you know, take up this house.

- As you devour me whole and destroy what's not needed in my life, rebuild me anew, take up this house. Queen of flesh, blood, and spirit take and guide me through the abyss so that I may conquer it, take up this house.

- IC ZSZSZS LIA ZIATU NAAMAH NAAMAH ZIATU!!!

* When you make the statement "Take up this house" take a sip of the wine you have set aside for yourself*

Opening the Gates of Naamah

Once the invocations have been completed, close your eyes and visualize a pit of fire that begins to encircle you. See the flames rise as high as possible. You may notice that the temperature in the temple may also begin to change, and it may become slightly warmer.

Now before you, see a black door appear. This door has the sigil of Naamah engraved in red. Stare at the sigil until it activates, once it activates the doors will open, and you are free to walk through to the other side. Once you've entered the door, you will most likely be greeted by Naamah in whatever form she chooses to present herself to you. From this point just let yourself go with the energies of the ritual.

Closing the Gates

Once you feel that you have gotten all that you can from the ritual, return through the gates and see them close before you. Afterward, give your thanks and your license to depart to Naamah and return to normal consciousness.

NOTE: Often times the practitioner may feel an intense sensation to masturbate while working with Naamah. If this is the case, do so and offer the sexual fluids to her by anointing her sigil.

-END

Chakra Dissolution Meditation

I suggest using this technique with caution; this meditation may unlock destructive and primal energies deep within you. My suggestion is to work through each chakra one at a time. Do not try to work from the Muladhara to the Sahasrara chakra in one sitting as it may prove to be too much for you. However, know that I am not telling you that you can't work through all the chakras at one time. I'm just suggesting that, if you do decide to work through them all in one go, at least, make sure that you have worked through the becoming darkness or the inverse breathing techniques first.

I discovered these techniques through my working with Tabris, a spirit associated with the 6th hour of the Nuctemeron. Her area of expertise is to unlock the essence of free will throughout the Magus's life. While working with her, I was led to techniques leading to the dissolution (destruction) of the chakras and freeing of very raw, primal forces trapped inside me. I chose only to tap into the seven commonly known chakras, I didn't go any deeper than that. Below I will include a brief description of the chakras, what elements they govern, their inverse elements and the techniques to dissolve them in darkness.

Muladhara/Root Chakra - Located at the base of the spine, it governs stability, foundation, safety, survival, the instinct to procreate. The most primal of energies of our lives are located here. The color associated with the Muladhara chakra is red.

The energies located here are very earthy and stabilizing. The seed sound associated with this chakra is LAM, the image of the Muladhara chakra is a red four petal lotus. This chakra houses the life changing, penetrative power of the kundalini. Earth is this chakras element.

Svadthisthana/Sacral Chakra - This chakra is located just below the navel, it governs our creativity, our center of balance, our intimacy and opened through the act of trust. The color of this chakra is orange, the energies here are very cool and soothing. The seed sound associated with this chakra is VAM. The image of the Svadthisthana is an orange six petal lotus. The element associated here is water.

Manipura/Solar Plexus Chakra - Living within the solar plexus, the Manipura gives us a sense of who we are through the act of willpower. It empowers our decisiveness and inner fires that often leads to physical action. This chakra is seen as a yellow ten-petal lotus. The seed sound associated is RAM and the element of fire fuels this chakra.

Anahata/Heart Chakra - Around the area of the heart, this chakra motivates us to either love or hate others. It activates when we are in a deep sense of peace, love, bliss, hate, even depression. When this chakra's center is opened, we speak with great emotional conviction and sincerity, giving us a sense of freedom.

The Anahatas is pictured as a green twelve-petaled lotus. The seed sound for this chakra is YAM. The Anahata element is air.

Vishuddha/Throat Chakra - Responsible for our verbal expression, the Vishuddha takes what we feel and communicates this with the world around us. Those that are great storytellers are usually lead and motivated by the energies of this chakra. It often pushes us towards very powerful and dynamic self-expression.

The element of the Vishuddah is aetheric. The image of a 16 petal lotus represents this chakra. The seed sound of the Vishuddha chakra is HAM.

Ajna/Third Eye - This chakra helps us to channel and develop our ability to see clearly astrally, magically and even physically. Sitting in the center of the forehead, once open, the Anja Chakra increases our clear and pristine vision. Making us more clairvoyant in the process. Tapping into the higher realms this chakra is great for projecting the will of the practitioner.

The Anja appears as an indigo colored two-petaled lotus. The element of this chakra is thought and the ability to project it into the world around us. The Anja seed sound is OM.

Sahasrara/Crown Chakra - The thousand petal lotus sitting at the very top of the head. This chakra governs the higher levels of ascension unlocking our true GOD/GODDESS potential. Here sits the seat of the creator, enabling us to take total control of our lives in its totality. The Sahasrara color is white and fueled by the essence of the all. The seed sound of this chakra is a combination of all the seeds sounds.

Now that you have a good understanding of the chakras we will go into the practice of dissolving the chakras.

MEDITATION:

Begin by sitting in complete darkness, start acclimating yourself to the surrounding darkness by performing either the "becoming darkness" or "inverse breathing" meditation. Once you feel that you have reached a state of complete emptiness within the darkness, take a few more deep cleansing breaths.

When ready, start visualizing the chakras as pools of spinning energy. See the chakras spinning in their respective colors at a speed and brightness that is comfortable for you. If you have to adjust the speed or the brightness until it feels right to feel free to do so.

Now switch your attention to cycling this same dark energy throughout each chakra starting at the Muladhara. Feel the expansion and contraction of the energy as it flows to, from and through the chakra empowers it. Penetrate each chakra this way with the same current of dark energy.

Next start visualizing each chakra's color slowly fading and taking on a blackened appearance. Make sure that you take your time and completely immerse each chakra with the energy of the darkness. Once that's achieved, envision that a black colored rod, staff or pipe shoots from the ground, up the spine, through each chakra and expands to the Sahasrara into the heavens above. This rod, staff or pipe will help you control the current of energy as it flows up and down your body.

Once you feel the energy of the chakra has changed, and that it has now taken on the shade of darkness return to the Muladhara chakra. While envisioning the Muladhara, begin chanting the seed sound in reverse. So instead of chanting the seed sound LAM you will then vibrate the seed sound as

MAL. As you do this, envision that the chakra is starting to dissolve, breaking apart and disappearing with each chant.

The chakra then becomes nothing but pure darkness in the process. At this moment, allow any energies and sensations that you feel overcome you. Let them devour you completely, don't fight the energies that are released let the surge do with you as it sees fit.

Explore each chakra in the same way by dissolving each one, one at a time. Take note of any spirits that may appear; any enns, sounds, colors, scents, emotions, reactions or thoughts that manifest during each dissolution. Let the energies control and move you in whatever way it desires, letting yourself succumb to the wave completely. Take as much time needed to work through each and every chakra, no need to rush to get to the Sahasrara chakra. As you move from the Muladhara, upwards use the rod as a vehicle to move the energy.

When you reach the Sahasrara chakra and it's been dissolved, let the energies radiate through your entire being and vibrating within the current of realized divine energies. Contract and expand this energy to and from yourself, feeling the push and pull of the very universe. Enjoy the waves of bliss and ecstasy that flow inside of you but don't get too caught up in it. This is the stage at which you learn to become truly detached from all things and have given into the darkness that is guiding and leading you.

When you have reached a state to where you are satisfied with what you have experienced, begin bringing yourself into normal consciousness. Start by reconstructing each chakra with light, begin with the Sahasrara chakra. Envision that the chakra is starting to reconstruct itself and returning to its intended state and color, shining brightly with a glorious light.

Pull this light energy downwards through the central pipe that connects each chakra. As the light travels through the pipe, visualize that it also begins to absorb the light and changes from a dark color to a light color. Perform this method with each chakra, rebuilding them with light energy that you are now re-absorbing into yourself. If it helps, light a single white candle when you are ready to start re-constructing the chakras.

Once the chakras have been reconstructed with light energy, start absorbing the light throughout your entire being. Starting with the space of darkness that you possessed, and then moving outwards to the bones, the tendons, the muscles, etc. When you have harmonized and balanced yourself within the light, take a few moments to let the energy settle itself. I don't suggest making any sudden movements after this meditation. Let the energy settle and ground.

I would like you to keep in mind that the key to this meditation is to go with the flow of the energy and not to fight it. If certain emotions, feelings, thoughts, pains, irritations, etc, appear just allow them to pass. When you dissolve the chakras, many blockages that may have kept you from ascending will also be dissolved.

The energies within this meditation have the tendency to swallow you within the abyss of your subconsciousness transforming you into your own personal God-form. But this truly can't happen until you achieve a state of non-attachment to all things.

*NOTE: Please take care when performing this meditation. The dark energies that you are awakening can have a tendency to put you in a very dark place. This is normal for this type of work, do know that this is all temporary and not permanent.

However, if you do reach a point to where things begin to spiral out of control for you seek some form of professional help.*

-END

Part 3: Opening The Gates to Manifest

TO MANIFEST

(*Laris ne na ca an vi no Colopatiron*)

The procedures and methods that I am about to discuss will go over physically parting the veil to the other side and opening spiritual gates. If you have an aversion to this type of ritual by all means, bypass this section.

Opening spiritual gates can be quite tricky. Especially if you are new to it, and have not grown used to the influx of energetic changes in the environment during regular invocations. It's really important that you ready yourself as much as possible, (see the section that refers to Preparation of the Practitioner) before attempting to open spiritual gates. These types of gates tend to not only part the veil to the other side, but it also opens you up as a living gate and conduit. If you aren't prepared, things such as fainting, frenzy, or unwanted entities occupying your space could happen.

In some cases, you may experience the manifestation of the Daemonic Divine. But it does all depend on how much energy and focus you put into the ritual. However, even though the chances of them physically manifesting may be very slim, that's not to say that it's not possible. That said, the energy that does radiate from the gates will be just as potent as if the Daemonic were standing right in front of you.

The reason you would open Daemonic gates in the first place would be to amplify the energy within the temple, giving you better results during and after your session. Every gate opens differently. You just have to add the right elements to the equation. Here are a few things that will help you in successfully opening your gates:

- Making sure that you are well rested and hydrated.

- Smudge the area with sage or dragon's blood to cleanse the space before and after opening any gates.

- Being abundant in energy.

- Remembering to mark your gate(s) physically.

- Guiding the flow of energy through each gate, with physical movement.

- Moving with the energetic flow of each gate.

- Spending 15 - 20 minutes opening each gate; If you fail to do so your gate(s) may not open.

- Opening your gate(s) before you start your meditation session to gain the best benefit.

- Considering using bodily fluids: If you were to use sexual fluids, blood, and saliva, it adds additional energy. Using them will add an extra boost of energy to your gate, too.

- Always close your gates after each session. This is a good way to get an unwanted guest to share your space with you if you don't. Never leave your gate(s) open.

- If you experience vomiting, nausea, fainting or any uncomfortable sensations, STOP!! you might not have the amount of energy needed to sustain yourself and open the gate(s) at the same time. If this does happen, wait at least four to five days then pick up where you left off.

Gate Opening Methods

Constructing your gate(s) can be done in any way that you see fit. But I've decided to go over a couple of gate opening construct methods below.

Pillar gate opening – This is created by setting the sigils on parchment (or whatever material you choose to use) up in a circular fashion wide enough for you to be able to sit inside of the pillar. Begin by drawing either the ZD sigil or the Seal of the Daemon over each paper sigil in the air while saying the Daemon's enn. You will have to perform this function several times until you feel the energy change in the temple, Trust me, it will.

After each gate has a sufficient amount of energy, perform a gesture that displays you opening the gate(s), do not forget this gesture for it is very powerful. To do this, place your hands together in front of you as if you are praying, then pull them open (to arms open wide) to simulate opening a gate. There are other gestures as well. If you are more comfortable with a different gesture, use that. Once the gates are opened, step into your pillar, have a seat and begin the meditation session. After you have completed your meditation, close your gate(s) completely.

Linear gate opening - This method can be used when you have only one individual gate to open. You will place your gate markers at a decent length in a line from each other. Perform the actions of drawing the ZD sigil or the seal of the Daemon over the sigils. As before, once you feel that a sufficient amount of energy has been built up, open the gate with a gate opening gesture. Once the gate has been opened, step through and begin your session.

Angular gate opening - This method is similar to the pillar gate opening except that you would use the angles of the circle to construct the gate. The same actions apply to this technique as well.

*NOTE: If you are choosing to meditate on a cushion or pillow make sure that it is physically on the other side of the gate. That way when you step through your gate, you will be ready to start your session.

Hopefully, this has given you a few ideas on gate opening methods. For more in-depth concepts, methods, and knowledge of gate opening, I recommend picking up S. Connolly's *"Infernal Colopatiron."* It will give you all that you need to know about working with spiritual gates and the spirits inside them.

Closing Your Gates

It's very important that when you have completed your work within each gate, you close them completely. As I stated before, you don't want any unwanted visitors slipping through unless you are ok with exploring the types of spiritual energies and entities that exists. And if that is the case, then go right ahead and leave the gates open. However, if gates are unattended, they can begin to take on a life of their own, making it difficult to close if you ever decided to do so.

The best method I have discovered for closing spiritual gates is to start by visualizing the energies being pushed back into the gates. This method also applies to the spirits that you were working with. Just make sure to give them thanks in the process. You would then perform a gate closing gesture as you do so you would then visualize the gate disappearing and dissipating into the ether.

Do this for every gate that you have open. Once you've closed all your gates feel free to smudge the area with dragon's blood and sage if need be. Make sure that just in case any wild energies do slip through that you have a good, powerful banishing on hand.

Daemon Reference

(Some Daemon references are courtesy of S. Connolly)

Here I've decided to add a list of Daemonic forces that are very capable of assisting you with your work. Feel free to add to the list or replace them with other God/Goddess forms. Be aware that this list is by no means complete. This list is just a small compilation of commonly, and maybe some uncommonly known Daemons that are experts in helping you understand and balance the nature of darkness inside of yourself.

Baalberith - Better known as the Prince of dying, rebirth and protection of the deceased. Baalberith can be worked with during periods of self-transformation.

- Direction: North
- Element: Earth
- Color: Black, gray
- Enn: Avage secore on ca Baalberith

Babael - Keeper of graves, Babael can cause a change to happen in a practitioner's life. He has even been considered a Daemon of dissolution.

- Direction: All
- Element: Earth
- Color: Gray
- Enn: Alan secore on ca Babael

Belial - Daemon of new beginnings and initiations, Belial is considered one of the nine divinities within the Dukante Daemonolatry hierarchy. Also worked with as an earth elemental when invoking ritual circles.

- Direction: North
- Element: Earth
- Color: Green, brown, black
- Enn: Lirach tasa vefa wehlc Belial

Eurynomous - Daemon of Death, rebirth, celebrations and new beginnings. Eurynomous carries with him the death current. He removes what's old and dead out of your life and replaces it with something of value.

- Direction: Northeast
- Element: Earth
- Colors: Black
- Enn: Ayar secore on ca Eurynomous

Flareous - A Daemon that creates action, causes love and passion that's ignited in a practitioner's life. Flareous is considered one of the nine divinities within the Dukante Daemonolatry hierarchy. Also worked with as a fire elemental when invoking ritual circles.

- Direction: South
- Element: Fire
- Color: Red, orange
- Enn: Ganic tasa fubin Flareous

Haagenti - Can make men wise. Causes alchemical transformations to take place in a person's life, usually altering ordinary and negative things and turning them into something great.

- Direction: Northwest
- Element: Earth, water
- Color: Orange
- Enn: Haagenti on ca lirach

Hahabi - Genius of fear, he is a perfect element for helping the practitioner conquer his/her personal fears

- Direction: South
- Element: Fire
- Color: Red
- Enn: Ami an ca tae vi no Hahabi

Hekate - Mother of the crossroads and the underworld

- Direction: All Directions
- Element: Earth, Water, (Some can even say abyssal)
- Color: Violet, Silver, Black
- Enn: Alora tasa Hekate borage et anana Hekate ayer at

Kali - Hindu Goddess and liberator of souls. Her energies are of freedom, death and change. Known by many names, Kali-ma destroys the ego and replaces it with truth beyond illusion.

- Direction: All
- Element: Chaos, The Abyss
- Colors: Black, Red
- Enn: Aum Kring Kalikaye Namaha

Leviathan - Often associated with healing, initiations, and emotions. Leviathan is considered one of the nine divinities within the Dukante Daemonolatry hierarchy. Also worked with as a water elemental when invoking ritual circles.

- Direction: West
- Element: Water
- Color: Blue, gray, black
- Enn: Jedan tasa hoet naca Leviathan

Lilith - First wife to Adam and mother of all demons. She is known as the queen of the night. Lilith empowers the practitioner through the current of death and transformation. She is also known to be the great revealer of knowledge.

- Direction: East, north
- Element: Air, earth, abyssal
- Color: Black, red, white
- Enn: Renich viasa avage Lilith lirach

Lucifer - Daemon of light and air, Lucifer creates a sense of freedom and wisdom whenever he is around.

- Direction: East
- Element: Air
- Colors: Yellow, white
- Enn: Renich tasa uberaca biasa icar Lucifer

Naamah - Mistress to Samael, sister to Lilith, Agrat Bat Mahlat, and Eisheth Zenunim. She has been considered to be the mother of all succubi.

- Direction: Some say West, however, I find that South West works even better
- Element: Water, fire, blood
- Color: Black, Red
- Enn: Ic Zs Zs Zs Lia Ziatu Naamah Naamah Ziatu

Satan - The All and the One. Satan is the King of the adversarial negative current.

- Direction: All
- Element: All
- Colors: All
- Enn: Tasa reme laris Satan- ave Satanas

Sigil Reference

(Some sigil references are courtesy of S. Connolly)

Baalberith

Babel

Belial

Eurynomous

Flareous

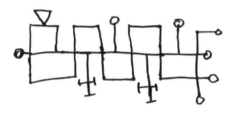

Haagenti

Hahabi

Hekate

Kali

Leviathan

Lilith

Lucifer

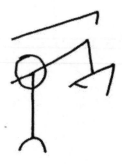

Naamah

Satan

Saturnian Sun Sigil

(*This is not the sigil of a particular entity*)

Afterword

Hopefully, inside of these pages you've found something that will help create some change in your life. I do wish you nothing but success in your spiritual progression. One thing that I've learned about spiritual progression is that it is a life-long journey and that it does take getting used to. But it is worth every single step.

Although these techniques may appear to be very simple, I do believe that they hold great power. These powerful energies have a possibility to awaken your true God self if managed properly. All you have to do is let the Daemonic Divine assist you in the process. I suggest becoming friends with these spirits, even the ones that may appear to you out of your personal darkness. They will prove to be the greatest spiritual allies that you work with. I also suggest finding the best way to utilize these changes and energies released during this working. Aim their energies towards something that will benefit you in the best possible way.

I hope that your spiritual fortitude increases and solidifies greatly. Through increased spiritual strength, you are bound to reach the next level on your path, putting you one step closer to becoming a Divine Being. These techniques have the ability to reveal your true God/Goddess self to you. If this does happen, take the time out to share your experience, knowledge and wisdom with others around you that have similar interests. Become charitable in your God/Goddess-hood so that we may all reach the same plateau one day.

I hope that through my work, you gain a chance to harmonize areas of your life that you may have found to be challenging. Eventually, you may notice that with this work your challenges will begin to melt away. I'm very appreciative of having been able to take charge of my life, and to mold it as I have seen fit through these methods and techniques. I wish that ultimately you will be able to gain the ability to penetrate through any obstacles that may stand in your way.

Overall, I would like to thank you for partaking in what I have to offer on the path of Ascension. I do hope that you have enjoyed the material provided in *"Divine Meditations: Mastering the Darkness Within."*

May Ashtaroth, Venus, and Belphagor bless you with sight, creativity, and fortune.

Bibliography & Recommended Reading

Connolly, S. Daemonolatry Goetia, 2009 DB Publishing

Connolly, S. The Daemonolater's Guide to Daemonic Magick 2009 DB Publishing

Connolly, S. Kasdeya Rite of Ba'al: Blood Rite of the Fifth Satan 2010 DB Publishing

Connolly, S. The Infernal Colopatiron, 2011-2012 DB Publishing

Hobbs Scott, E. Gates of Lucifer, 2014 DB Publishing

TO EXPERIENCE, TO SEEK, TO BE SILENT, TO DARE, TO KNOW, TO WILL, TO MANIFEST

NOTES

More from DB Publishing & Official Melissa Press

By S. Connolly

- The Complete Book of Demonolatry
- The Daemonolater's Guide to Daemonic Magick
- The Art of Creative Magick
- Daemonolatry Goetia
- Infernal Colopatiron or Abyssal Angels: Redux
- Curses, Hexes & Crossings: A Magician's Guide to Execration Magick
- Honoring Death: The Arte of Daemonolatry Necromancy
- Necromantic Sacraments
- Kasdeya Rite of Ba'al: Blood Rite of the Fifth Satan
- Nuctemeron Gates
- Abyssal Communion & Rite of Imbibement
- Keys of Ocat
- Drawing Down Belial
- Bound By Blood: Musings of a Daemonolatress

By M. Delaney

- Sanctus Quattuordecim: Daemonolatry Sigil Magick

By E. Purswell

- Goetic Demonolatry

By Martin McGreggor

- Paths to Satan

Various Authors (Compilation Books)

- My Name is Legion: For We Are Many
- Demonolatry Rites
- Ater Votum: Daemonolatry Prayer
- Satanic Clergy Manual

Workbooks and Journals by S. Connolly

- The Goetia Workbook
- 30 Days of Spirit Work
- The Spirit Workbook
- The Meditation Journal
- Ritus Record Libri

Made in the USA
Coppell, TX
22 May 2021